The Country Life Picture Book of
Royal London

The Country Life Picture Book of
Royal London

Gordon Winter

COUNTRY LIFE BOOKS

frontispiece
Trooping the Colour. Every year, on the Saturday in
June nearest to her official birthday, Her Majesty the
Queen, accompanied by a Sovereign's Escort of the
Household Cavalry, reviews her Foot Guards on the
Horse Guards Parade. We in Britain are fortunate that
we have a monarch who rides not only astride but, as
she is required to do on this occasion, side-saddle, with
exceptional grace and skill.

COUNTRY · LIFE
NEWNES·BOOKS

Newnes, itself founded in 1881, purchased
Country Life magazine in 1897. Books were an
important part of the business and more than
eight hundred titles were published prior to
1947. Today Country Life books are published
on many subjects including Architecture,
Natural History, British Heritage, Antiques and
Equestrian sport. Some, such as the Dictionary
of English Furniture, first published in 1924, are
still in print. Sister imprints include Collingridge
and Temple Press Books.

Published by Country Life Books,
an imprint of Newnes Books,
Astronaut House, Feltham, Middlesex, England
and distributed for them by
The Hamlyn Publishing Group Limited
Rushden, Northants, England.

© Gordon Winter 1983

First published 1983

ISBN 0 600 36843 2

Printed in Italy

Introduction

At what point in history did London first become a royal city? To that question there can be no positive answer. No Alexander thrust his spear into a chosen point on the northern shore of the Thames, exclaiming: 'Here shall men build a great city'. There is, however, no doubt that London was a Roman foundation. Before the Roman invasions there was possibly no human settlement at all, where London now stands; only tidal marshes on the south side of the river, and woodland, probably with grassy clearings, on the gravel banks that marked the northern shore.

It is in fact current archaeological doctrine that, before the Romans, there were no towns in Britain anywhere. That view is at least open to argument. It depends on what is meant by the word town. There can be no doubt that there were no cities in Britain until the Romans built them. But town is a looser definition. The inhabitants of south-eastern Britain, who met that first Roman reconnaissance-in-force in 55 BC, and Claudius's invasion and occupation a hundred years later, were far removed from the painted savages that folk-legend suggests. They had a highly developed Celtic civilisation of their own, producing magnificent art and ornament, and a well-organised war-machine. Their iron-age hill-forts remain all over southern England, as impressive as any feats of engineering that the Romans have left, south of Hadrian's Wall. They were successful and enterprising farmers, and have left enough traces of their wooden barns and houses to establish that they did not live, and did not need to live, in primitive hovels.

Unfortunately the British were not literate, and have left us with no written record to match and rectify those disparaging accounts by Caesar and later Roman journalist-historians, whose writing was as likely to be tinged with propaganda as other war-reporters' accounts have been ever since.

Why, then, was London built where it now stands? The Catuvellauni, who ruled south-eastern Britain before Caesar's invasion, saw no need for a town, or a fortress, on the wet, wild and unproductive shores of the river where the Romans built their provincial capital. What factors governed the Romans' choice?

Probably the British had fords, and possibly regular ferries, across the Thames in the London region before the Romans landed; and Roman intelligence and reconnaissance, carried out long before each invasion, would have discovered where those fords and ferries were. The British already had rough roads of a sort, and they may have had a regular crossing-place somewhere near Westminster, or where London Bridge now stands. What we have to remember is that the Romans were not bringing their army into a trackless waste, but into a farmed and settled countryside, even though it was still sparsely settled.

It would be pleasant to suppose that, before the Romans came, there were at least small British settlements at those crossing places, because we could then claim that London existed as a British foundation before it became a Roman capital. The locations of Westminster or London Bridge have been suggested as likely for several reasons. Westminster may have been the point furthest down-stream at which the Thames was fordable. And Westminster, or the London Bridge area, may have been approximately where the river ceased to be tidal. Both are several miles below their present-day equivalents, but that is what we would expect. For very many centuries the land of south-east England has been falling in relation to sea-level. In Roman times it is thought that the land at what is now London Bridge was some 15 feet higher in relation to high-tide levels. In other words the river would have been 15 feet shallower than it now is at Westminster; and the tide would not have run so far upstream.

But, argue the archaeologists, if there were permanent British crossing places at Westminster, or at the site of London Bridge, it should be possible to find pre-Roman coins, and Celtic pottery, at those places. No such finds have been made, indeed they are conspicuously absent. Does that argument not overlook the 15-foot change in the depth of the river? Might not the Thames have been much narrower at that time than we are inclined to suppose? Might not the missing coins and potsherds lie deep in the mud, well below the present low-tide marks?

Whatever the truth, the Romans were not slow to recognise that the site of London was a natural centre of communications for anyone who aspired to rule

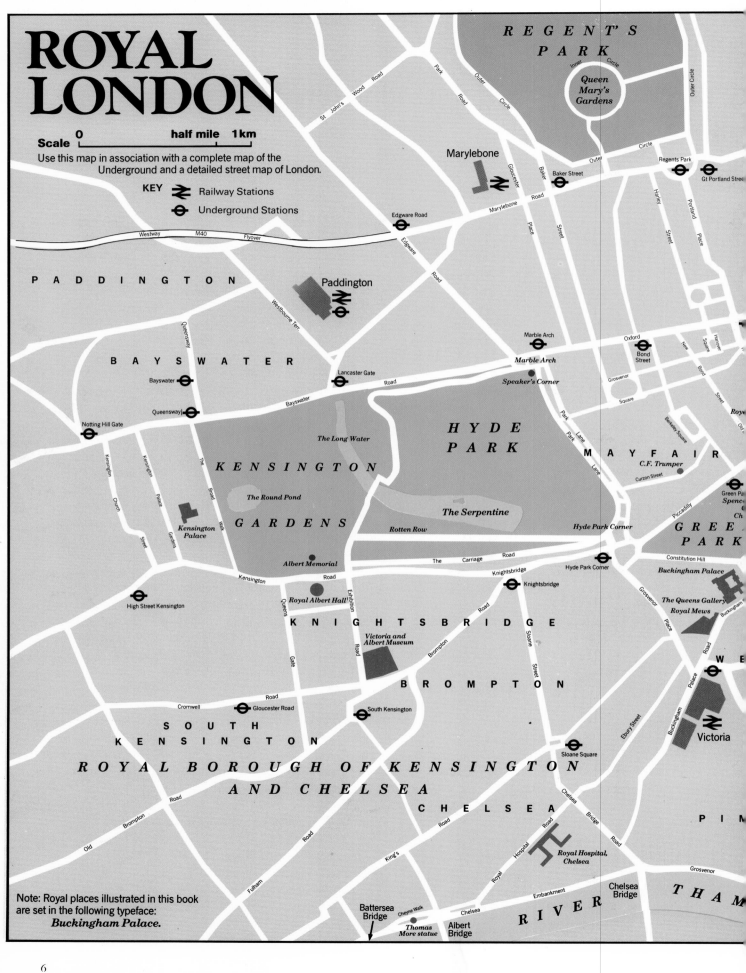

ROYAL LONDON

Scale 0 — half mile — 1km

Use this map in association with a complete map of the Underground and a detailed street map of London.

KEY ⟩⟩ Railway Stations

⊖ Underground Stations

REGENT'S PARK

Queen Mary's Gardens

Marylebone

Baker Street

Regents Park

Gt Portland Street

Edgware Road

Marylebone Road

Westway   M40   Flyover

PADDINGTON

Paddington

Marble Arch

Oxford

Bond Street

Marble Arch

Speaker's Corner

BAYSWATER

Bayswater

Lancaster Gate

Bayswater Road

Grosvenor Square

HYDE PARK

MAYFAIR

Queensway

Notting Hill Gate

The Long Water

C.F. Trumper

Curzon Street

KENSINGTON

The Round Pond

The Serpentine

Green Park Spencer Ch

The Round Pond

GARDENS

Rotten Row

Hyde Park Corner

GREEN PARK

Kensington Palace

Albert Memorial

The Carriage Road

Constitution Hill

Buckingham Palace

Kensington Road

Hyde Park Corner

Knightsbridge

Knightsbridge

The Queens Gallery

Royal Mews

High Street Kensington

Royal Albert Hall

KNIGHTSBRIDGE

Victoria and Albert Museum

BROMPTON

WE

Cromwell Road

Gloucester Road

South Kensington

Victoria

SOUTH KENSINGTON

Sloane Square

ROYAL BOROUGH OF KENSINGTON

AND CHELSEA

CHELSEA

PIM

Brompton Road

Old Brompton Road

Fulham Road

King's Road

Royal Hospital, Chelsea

Chelsea Bridge

Grosvenor

Note: Royal places illustrated in this book are set in the following typeface:
Buckingham Palace.

Battersea Bridge

Cheyne Walk

Chelsea

Thomas More statue

Albert Bridge

RIVER THAM

Chelsea Bridge

6

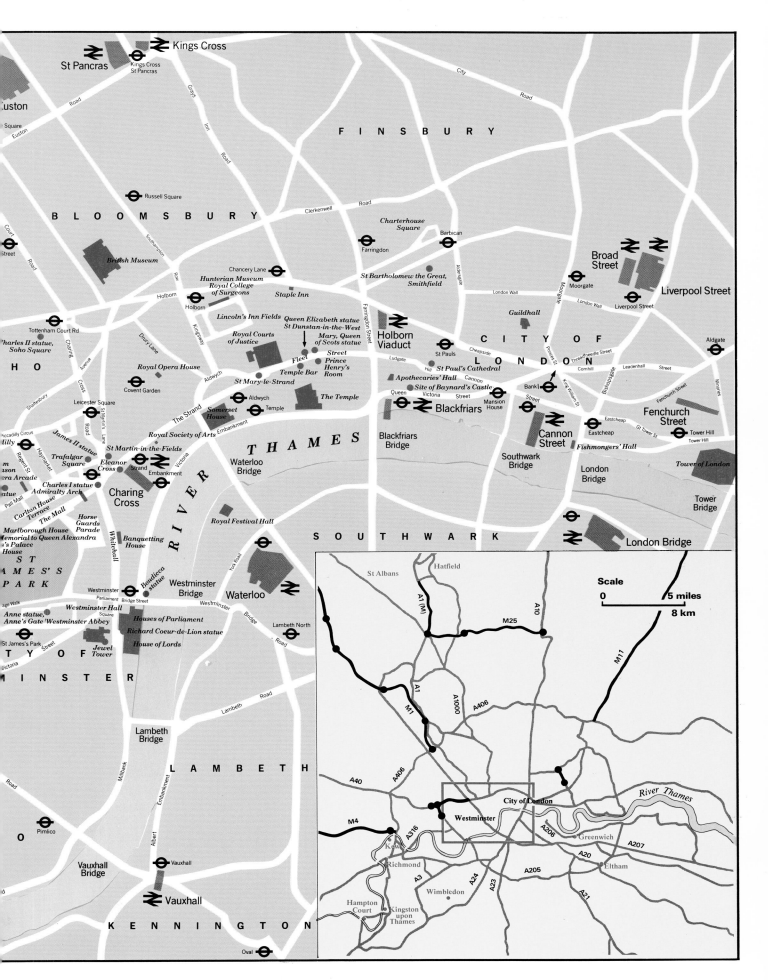

St Pancras

Kings Cross
Kings Cross
St Pancras

Euston
Square

Euston

Euston Road

Grays
Inn
Road

City
Road

F I N S B U R Y

Russell Square

B L O O M S B U R Y

Court
Street

Euston
Road

Southampton
Row

Clerkenwell   Road

Charterhouse
Square

Barbican

Broad
Street

Liverpool Street

British Museum

Farringdon

London Wall

Moorgate

Moorgate

Liverpool Street

Charles II statue,
Soho Square

S O
H O

Tottenham Court Rd

Charing

Holborn

Holborn

Chancery Lane

Hunterian Museum
Royal College
of Surgeons

Staple Inn

Kingsway

Lincoln's Inn Fields

Royal Courts
of Justice

Queen Elizabeth statue
St Dunstan-in-the-West

Mary, Queen
of Scots statue

St Bartholomew the Great,
Smithfield

Farringdon Street

Holborn
Viaduct

C I T Y   O F   L O N D O N

Aldersgate

London Wall

Guildhall

Aldgate

Cross

Avenue

Drury Lane

Royal Opera House

Covent Garden

Aldwych

Fleet   Street

Temple Bar

St Mary-le-Strand

Prince
Henry's
Room

Ludgate

Cheapside

St Pauls

St Paul's Cathedral

Apothecaries' Hall

Cannon

Princes St.

Cornhill

Threadneedle Street

Leadenhall   Street

Bishopsgate

Aldgate

Shaftesbury

Leicester Square

St Martin's Lane

The Strand

Aldwych

Temple

The Temple

Queen   Victoria

Site of Baynard's Castle

Bank

King William St.

Street

Mansion
House

Blackfriars

Fenchurch Street

Piccadilly Circus

James II statue

Regent St.

Haymarket

Trafalgar
Square

Royal Society of Arts

Eleanor
Cross

St Martin-in-the-Fields

Somerset
House

Victoria

Embankment

Blackfriars
Bridge

Southwark
Bridge

Cannon
Street

Eastcheap

Eastcheap

Fishmongers' Hall

Gt Tower St.

Fenchurch
Street

Tower Hill

Tower Hill

Piccadilly

Charles I statue
Admiralty Arch

Charing
Cross

Strand

Embankment

Waterloo
Bridge

T H A M E S

R I V E R

S O U T H W A R K

London
Bridge

Tower of London

son
era Arcade
statue

Pall Mall

Carlton House
Terrace

The Mall

Horse
Guards
Parade

Royal Festival Hall

London Bridge

Tower
Bridge

Marlborough House
Memorial to Queen Alexandra
's Palace
House

S T
A M E S 'S
P A R K

Whitehall

Banquetting
House

York Road

S O U T H W A R K

Anne statue,
Anne's Gate

Boudicca
statue

Westminster
Bridge

Westminster

Parliament   Bridge Street

Westminster Hall

Houses of Parliament

Waterloo

Waterloo

Lambeth North

age Walk

Westminster
Square

Richard Coeur-de-Lion statue

House of Lords

St James's Park

Jewel
Tower

Bridge

Lambeth   Road

T Y   O F
M I N S T E R

Westminster Abbey

St James's
Street

Victoria

L A M B E T H

Lambeth
Bridge

Millbank

Embankment

Lambeth   Road

Road

O

Pimlico

Vauxhall
Bridge

Albert   Embankment

Vauxhall

Vauxhall

K E N N I N G T O N

Oval

The East Front of Buckingham Palace: a ceremonial
occasion. When John Nash largely rebuilt Buckingham
House for George IV, he designed it to face the other
way round, so that his West Front of Bath stone
overlooked the gardens, which were designed by
Aiton. This very elegant side of the Palace is not
normally seen by the public. The present East Front,
which is what most of us know of the Palace, was
added for George V and Queen Mary by Aston Webb
as recently as 1913.

Britain. The tidal Thames gave easy access by sea to
the European continent, which Rome already ruled,
and river access deep inland as far as present-day
Gloucestershire. It was the furthest point downstream
at which the river could readily be crossed. And on the
north shore, nature had provided the additional
advantage of a high and extensive bank of gravel.

In Roman times we can only marginally claim that
London was royal. Claudius was an emperor; but his
foundation and rule were at one remove, through
provincial governors.

British royalty does not appear on the London scene
until the coming of Boudicca (or Boadicea) in AD 61,
and that occasion was hardly constructive. Boudicca's
army, reckoned to total some 250,000 men, sacked and
destroyed London as they had sacked Verulamium and

Colchester, killing between 70,000 and 80,000 Roman
settlers before they were finally defeated in a day-long
battle by a small Roman force of perhaps 10,000 men
under Suetonius.

That first London must have been mainly of wood.
In his splendid book, *Londinium*, published
posthumously and revised by Sarah Macready, Dr John
Morris, of London University, writes: 'In Colchester,
London and Verulamium, in the town centres and
adjoining streets, a thick layer of burnt debris covers
pottery and coins dated earlier than AD 60. In London,
many dozens of skulls, with few other bones, were
reported from the bed of the Walbrook, mostly
concentrated between Finsbury Circus and the south
side of London Wall . . .'

From its rapid rebuilding after the defeat of

Boudicca's rebellion, London developed into one of the major provincial capitals of the Roman Empire. Its citizens grew wealthy, as they have done in later ages, from Londinium's dual role as seat of government and principal sea-port. For over three centuries, until about AD 400, London enjoyed an era of peace and prosperity that it has scarcely equalled since. It also acquired stout walls, parts of which remain, which stood it in good stead in the troubled years after the collapse of Roman power at the beginning of the 5th century. Britain was then left to fend for herself against the barbarian invaders, and though there were Romano-British kings or emperors, who doubtless ruled from London, we know little about them.

No great name emerges until nearly the end of the 5th century, when Arthur, once thought of as a legendary figure but now re-established as a Romano-British sovereign, Artorius, won a great victory at Badon, near Bath, over the Saxon, or English, invaders. Arthur largely restored Romano-British rule; John Morris describes him with a fine flourish as 'the last Roman emperor of Britain', of which London was still possibly the official capital.

After Arthur's final defeat in battle, of which we know only that it took place, his kingdom broke into warring fragments. By the end of the 6th century the British, with their surviving language, had retreated to Wales and Cornwall, and the whole of England was in Anglo-Saxon hands. The next effective royal ruler of London, Aethelbert of Kent, had no more than the south-eastern corner of the island to govern from his forlorn capital. It must have been hard for the surviving Londoners, who had learnt by word-of-mouth of the splendour of their city only a few generations earlier, to foresee the even greater splendour that was to come.

Roman London in its prime was no more than a tenth the size of Rome, but it was a great and important city nonetheless. As in most other Roman cities in Britain, little of it has survived above ground. Succeeding generations, in a poorer age, had no use for the crumbling monuments of empire; palatial buildings, public and private alike, degenerated into convenient quarries for stone and brick. What did

survive, because they continued to meet a need, were the Walls. Solidly built of Kentish ragstone, with a few bonding-courses of red tiles, the Roman Walls of London probably rose to a height of twenty feet or more, tapering slightly upwards from a base about eight feet thick. They were probably built in the very late 2nd or early 3rd century AD.

These defences remained in use right down to Tudor times, with periodic repairs and additions by the later Roman authorities, by Alfred the Great, by the Normans, and by various medieval defenders down to the Wars of the Roses. Edward IV added a brick curtain wall, with stone-silled embrasures, when Queen Margaret and the Lancastrians were advancing on London.

In AD 604, seven years after St Augustine landed in Kent to bring Christianity to the English, he consecrated Mellitus as Bishop of London, and the first cathedral church of St Paul was built. The city became increasingly important from that time onwards. During the Viking raids of the 9th century, London suffered heavily when it was attacked in 842 and again in 851. It was finally occupied by the Danes, but was liberated in 886 by Alfred the Great, who restored the Walls and reorganised the defences.

It is from 886 that the story of royal London, in the modern sense, can be said to have begun. The men of London formed an important part of Alfred's army during his final victorious campaigns against the Danes in Essex (893–896), and the Anglo-Saxon Chronicle records that captured Viking ships, if still serviceable, were brought to London. For most of the 10th century, London enjoyed peace and growing prosperity, but from 980 onwards, Viking raids were renewed, in the disastrous reign of Ethelred ('the Unready' or better, 'the ill-advised'). On many occasions the armed citizens of London were strong enough to beat off the Danes, but in 1013, when the Danish king Swein had overrun the whole country, London had to submit. Swein, however, died early in the next year, and Ethelred came back from his refuge in Normandy. According to the saga of St Olaf, the King of Norway helped Ethelred to recapture London in a spectacular river-battle, at the height of which

London Bridge was pulled down by the Norse ships.
This is folklore rather than history, but Olaf's memory
is still preserved in St Olave's, Hart Street, and in
Tooley (St Olave's) Street, Southwark. Some writers
claim that the event is recalled in the children's song,
London Bridge is Broken Down.

When Ethelred died, in 1016, his son Edmund
Ironside was chosen as king with the support of the
Londoners. He soon justified their confidence by
raising a prolonged siege, driving the Danes back to
their ships, and again defeating them in a great battle
at Brentford. At Ashingdon in Essex, however,
Edmund's army was defeated through treachery, and
he was forced to divide the country with the new
Danish king, Canute. In November Edmund died, and
from 1016 to 1035 Canute ruled all England as well as
Denmark. London's wealth at that time is shown by
the huge tax paid by the citizens in 1018, when Canute
wanted to pay off his fleet. London paid 10,500 pounds
of silver, compared with 72,000 pounds from all the
rest of England. Now, at least, with a Danish king on
the throne, London could trade freely with all the
German and Baltic ports, and many Danish merchants
added to its prosperity. St Clement Danes seems to
preserve a memory of that period.

After Canute's death in 1035, he was succeeded
briefly by two sons, Harald and Harthacanute, and
finally by Harthacanute's half-brother Edward the
Confessor. Edward, who had lived in Normandy,
brought many French-speaking Normans to London
with him. They were not well received by the
Londoners, and Edward withdrew to Thorney Island,
upsteam at Westminster. At Westminster, earlier Saxon
Kings had built a church to St Peter, which had
become a Benedictine monastery, and here Edward
established his court, and devoted his energies to the
building of an Abbey church. He was too ill to attend
the consecration of his Abbey before his death in 1065,
and he was buried there near the High Altar.

In 1053 Harold, son of Godwin, Canute's former
adviser, had succeeded his father as Earl of Wessex and
adviser to Edward, so at Edward's death Harold was
proclaimed King, with the support of the City of
London, and was crowned in Westminster Abbey, the
first English king to be crowned there.

That, however, was only the beginning of his
troubles. Harold Hardrada, King of Norway, landed to
claim the crown, with the support of Harold's brother
Tostig, and Harold marched north to defeat them at
Stamford Bridge. Meanwhile the bastard Duke
William of Normandy, with only a very spurious claim
to the throne, landed in Sussex, and Harold marched
south again to meet him, picking up on the way a
strong contingent of London's citizen-soldiers. When
Harold was killed and the English army defeated, some
of the citizen-soldiers were able to withdraw to
London, where the boy, Edgar the Atheling, of
Alfred's line, had been proclaimed king.

Had the English united they might still have
defeated William, but the great earls, jealous among
themselves, hesitated to join London in opposing the
Normans. Finally the Londoners, after long
negotiation, came to terms and William was
proclaimed king.

William was too shrewd a man to forget that he
could not rule England without the support of
London. Two years after he was crowned, he gave the
City a charter, still preserved. Translated into modern
English it reads: 'William the king greets William the
bishop, Geoffrey the Portreeve and all the citizens
within London, both French and English, in friendly
wise. And I give you to know that ye be all law-
worthy as ye were in King Edward's time. And I will
that every child shall be his father's heir after his
father's day, and I will suffer no man to do you
wrong. God keep you.'

Only in very loose terms could that slip of
parchment be described as a charter. But at least it was
a statement of intent, and set the pattern for relations
between monarch and City for many reigns to come.
William had behind him his personal mystique as
crowned king, and his personal forces, together with
those of his Norman lords that he could call upon
when needed, though neither the lords nor their
soldiers were reliable. London, on the other hand, had
great and growing wealth. It also had a closely knit
and well-trained body of soldier-citizens, serving not
under feudal obligation but as free men in their own

cause. The size of London's army is surprising. Fitzstephen, Thomas à Becket's secretary, writing later but still of Norman London, put the City forces at 20,000 cavalry and 60,000 foot, though he may have exaggerated.

The commencement of the building of the Tower of London by William was therefore intended for national defence and also to strengthen his own position in relation to the City. He began the keep of the fortress, the White Tower, in 1078, and it was finished by his son, William Rufus. Rufus added a curtain wall and moat, though the whole fortress still takes its name from the Conqueror's keep. The White Tower remains largely as the two Williams built it, and is one of the best surviving examples of Norman defensive architecture in the whole of England. The most important changes since it was built are the large windows put in by Christopher Wren 600 years later.

The King maintained another residence and fortress in the City, Baynard's Castle, designed to defend the south-western corner of the river frontage, as the Tower guarded the south-east. But his principal residence, continuing Edward the Confessor's example, was at the Palace of Westminster, and it was here that William Rufus built the great Westminster Hall, added to by Richard II and still surviving as one of London's principal Norman monuments.

Even by the Conqueror's time little can have remained of Roman London except for the Walls, and the Roman gates. Within the gates the pattern of Roman planned thoroughfares, which those gates fitted, had disappeared and been replaced by a jumble of wooden buildings along narrow and winding streets. There were also areas of open space – perhaps waste ground but more probably cultivated as market gardens. Fitzstephen, writing in praise of London, recorded that the City's gardens were spacious and beautiful, well furnished with trees; and there were fields for pasture, though it is not clear whether any of these were within the Walls.

The City of London owned or controlled much land beyond the City Walls. Epping Forest belonged to the City in Norman times, as it still does; more surprisingly London controlled Middlesex, by virtue

of a charter granted by Henry I in 1139 which empowered the City to appoint the Sheriff.

London's first mayor (the title did not become Lord Mayor until the reign of Henry VII) was Henry Fitz-Eylwin, a name that survives as FitzAlan, who held office not for a year but from 1191 to his death in 1212. By then the power of London, though effectively still in the hands of the great merchant princes, was becoming formalised through the craft-guilds who nominated the mayor. These guilds were in some ways not unlike trades unions; they ensured that only members could practice certain trades and crafts, and they set wage levels; unlike some modern trades unions, however, they insisted on maintaining high standards of work. Many of the guilds or companies survive, though few retain their ancient powers. The Goldsmith's Company still puts its mark on gold articles, and the Apothecaries Company still grants licences, as does the Company of Watermen and Lightermen.

Throughout the Middle Ages London remained a walled city, though for long periods the Walls were neglected and then hastily repaired at times of danger, as in the Wars of the Roses. By the 15th century, however, the area within the Walls was becoming overcrowded, and rich men were beginning to move out to the open country between the City and Westminster. Partly by the normal process of change and rebuilding, and partly because of the effect of the Great Fire of 1666, little of medieval London remains, but some glimpses of what it was like can be seen in Guildhall, and in Grays Inn and Lincolns Inn, with houses built round a courtyard reached through a communal gateway. Crosby Hall, the home of the wealthy merchant, Sir John Crosby, on the east side of Bishopsgate, in what is still called Crosby Square, has survived because it was taken to pieces and reconstructed near Chelsea Old Church, on the site of the Chelsea home of Sir Thomas More, who had once lived at Crosby Hall as had, briefly, Richard III.

Like successful monarchs before him, Henry VII was at pains to keep on good terms with London; and the City, now spreading far beyond its Walls, flourished in the Tudor age. Henry VIII's Dissolution of the

Monasteries had a severe effect, however, because the disappearance of the religious houses caused unemployment and at the same time removed the institutions that had done most to care for the poor. Some monastic buildings were put to new uses; others were gradually pulled down to provide materials for new buildings. Most are remembered now only in names like Charterhouse, Whitefriars and Blackfriars. Somerset House, the Beaufort palace between the river and the road to Westminster, was said to have been built with stone from six different monasteries. Other such houses are remembered now only in names of streets built when the houses in their turn gave way to new buildings. West of Somerset House, the five parts of the name of George Villiers, Duke of Buckingham, were once remembered in five streets around Adelphi, even including an 'Of Alley' until some dimwit in County Hall, missing the point, changed Of Alley to its present dull York Place.

Beyond the Walls, down river at Deptford and at Woolwich, two new royal dockyards were opened for the expanding Navy. At Greenwich the Palace of Placentia, (later rebuilt by Wren as the Royal Naval Hospital, Greenwich) was a principal Tudor residence, and was the birthplace of Elizabeth I.

Henry VIII's most enduring contribution to London is St James's Palace, though little remains of the Tudor fabric except for the fine brick Gatehouse on St James's Street. The reign of Elizabeth I has left surprisingly few London landmarks. Yet she attempted a most significant reform which foreshadowed the modern concept of the Green Belt. Seeing the need for open space for the citizens of a rapidly expanding metropolis, she prohibited, in 1580, any new building within three miles of the Walls. Alas, the prohibition did not last for long. Surviving from her reign, however, are two important great halls of the Inns of Court: those of Grays Inn and Middle Temple. It was in these two halls that Shakespeare's *Comedy of Errors* (1594) and *Twelfth Night* (1602) were given their first performances.

Only under the Stuarts did London begin to acquire enough surviving landmarks for a man or woman of that era to be able to recognise some of them today.

Notable are Inigo Jones's Banqueting House in Whitehall, his Queen's House at Greenwich, and St Paul's, Covent Garden. The whole of the Covent Garden piazza was designed by him for the Earl of Bedford in 1631. Kensington Palace, though it began life as a private house in 1605, became a royal palace when it was bought by William III in 1689, and it has remained a favourite royal residence ever since. But it was the Great Fire of 1666 which gave Wren and other architects their opportunity to rebuild. Wren and Evelyn, encouraged by Charles II, both drew up projects for a splendid new London, with wide, straight thoroughfares and elegant public buildings. For a year or so it seemed that London might become once again the planned, classical city that it was in Roman times, but conflicting interests between the City Corporation, Parliament and Crown, together with the physical difficulty of clearing the rubble, led to a continuation of the haphazard and piecemeal building that has given London its distinctive character. Wren's Royal Avenue, designed to reach Kensington Palace, got no further than the King's Road. But at least the rebuilding left London with St Paul's cathedral, the masterpiece of English baroque, with Wren's splendid 'hospitals' for retired soldiers and sailors at Chelsea and Greenwich, and with the astonishing total of fifty-four Wren churches to replace some of the eighty-nine churches destroyed in the Great Fire. The role of Charles II in aiding and encouraging Wren is too little appreciated; but for him St Paul's cathedral itself might have been scaled down from its present grandeur.

Parts of London, at least, assumed the appearance of a planned city in Georgian times. The growth of London between 1714 and 1808 made it the largest city in the world, with a dominating influence not only politically but economically, for the simple reason that (as George Rudé points out in *Hanoverian London*) in 1750 one Englishman in ten lived in London, compared with perhaps one Frenchman in 40 then living in Paris. As Rudé puts it: 'The Jacobite challenge had been finally defeated, and the landed classes, relatively undivided, shared the spoils of office, built their squares and terrace houses, and basked in social and religious peace'.

The Tower of London as the Normans never saw it. Most places with white in their name, like Whitehall and the many Whitchurches, are so called because their new-cut stones looked white when they were built; but William the Conqueror's White Tower acquired its name because Henry III actually had it covered in whitewash. In the foreground is Tower Bridge, now as much a landmark as the Tower itself.

London's Georgian terraces and squares reflect that prosperity and stability, and still offer the most sought after and admired of her private houses.

Of all the architectural embellishments of London that were made with royal encouragement during the Victorian era, the most important was surely the Crystal Palace. For the Great Exhibition of 1851, held in Hyde Park under the guiding hand of the Prince Consort, Joseph Paxton's brilliant structure of glass and iron, in prefabricated section, was far ahead of its time. If English architecture had followed the lead that Paxton had given, it could have anticipated by many decades the work of the Bauhaus, of le Corbusier and of Frank Lloyd Wright. But alas, English architects of the 19th century looked backward rather than forward for their inspiration, and dissipated their energy in the great debate between the champions of the Classical and the Gothic revival. Philip Hardwick's splendid Doric arch – now, alas, demolished – at Euston Station can hardly be said to have been looking into the future, but it was much admired in the 1830s; and even St Pancras station, built by George Gilbert Scott nearly two decades after the Crystal Palace, was still trying to be a cathedral rather than a railway terminus. The Crystal Palace was moved to Sydenham in 1853 but was destroyed by fire in 1936 – a tragic loss.

It is one of London's many anomalies that though the English are the world's masters at the staging of ceremonial processions (the wedding of the Prince of Wales and Lady Diana Spencer is the most recent example of that pre-eminence) the capital has only one processional way, and that, in chronological terms, is almost an afterthought. Of the two architectural features that terminate the Mall, the Portland stone East Front of Buckingham Palace was added in 1913, and the Admiralty Arch was built as part of the National Memorial to Queen Victoria in 1910.

The Mall is not only a ceremonial way. It provides the theatrical setting, on appropriate occasions, for the people of London to express their personal loyalty to the Sovereign, and for the Sovereign to acknowledge that loyalty from the balcony of the Palace. The close link between the Crown and the capital has existed, almost unbroken, for a thousand years. During the Second World War, at the height of the Blitz, the sense of security and stability which the presence of the Sovereign gives to Londoners was expressed in a popular song, which found favour while the bombs were falling. The words of the chorus were: 'The King is still in London'.

Gordon Winter.

Boadicea as Londoners remember her. Boadicea's, or Boudicca's, contribution to the first Roman London was to destroy it totally; however, it is interesting to reflect that, but for the misrule of the Roman Empire by Nero and those who governed in his name, the Iceni might never have been goaded into their famous rebellion, which came so near to throwing the invading Romans back into the sea only eighteen years after the conquest in AD 43. (See page 8.)

Kingston-on-Thames: the Coronation Stone. In the
10th century, after Alfred the Great and his son
Edward had re-united the Danelaw with the rest of
England, English kings were crowned at Kingston.
Among them were Alfred's grandson, Athelstan;
Athelstan's brother, Edmund the Magnificent,
murdered at a banquet; Edward the Martyr, who
inherited the crown when he was twelve and was
murdered when he was sixteen; and Ethelred the
Redeless (which means that he was ill-advised, not
unready). (See page 9.)

Westminster Abbey (*opposite*). Edward the Confessor would not recognise now the monastic church or 'minster' that he built in the 'west', between about 1050 and 1065 on what was then Thorney, or Thorne Island. That the site ever was an 'island', surrounded by Thames backwaters, can be seen from a modern drawing, hanging in the Abbey of what it was probably like. Most of the present building is 13th century and later.

Weepers on the tomb of Edward III (*right, top*), also in the chapel of Edward the Confessor. The monument is by Master Henry Yevele; it consists of an altar tomb of Purbeck marble, and the weepers are of bronze. They represent six children of Edward III. Those shown are, from the left, the Black Prince, Joan de la Tour and Lionel, Duke of Clarence.

The tomb of Queen Eleanor of Castile in Westminster Abbey (*right, bottom*). The gilt-bronze effigy, made by William Torel in 1291, is in Edward the Confessor's chapel, that is to say between Henry VII's chapel and the High Altar. Queen Eleanor's right hand once held a sceptre; the left hand is closed over the string of her cloak. The gilt-bronze tomb-top, and the crossed pillows beneath her head, are decorated with the Castle of Castile and the Lion of León

Westminster Abbey: fan vaulting and pendants on the roof of Henry VII's chapel. Built between 1503 and 1512, the chapel is the latest part of the medieval Abbey. Pevsner, in his *London: Volume I*, of *The Buildings of England*, writes of it: 'The wealth of detail, especially at the chancel end, defeats description. Technically it is a spectacular tour de force.' Pevsner also remarks that Westminster Abbey is 'the most French of all English Gothic churches'.

The Palace of Westminster: the Jewel Tower (*below*).
The tower, built for the security of the King's treasury,
as its name suggests, is the only surviving reminder
that the Palace of Westminster, though never as strong
as the Tower of London, was once fortified. This
tower, guarding the south-west corner, was built in
1364-66 but the windows are 18th-century. Its moat is
a survival of the water-defences of Thorne Island, on
which the Palace of Westminster was built.

The Palace of Westminster: Westminster Hall
(*opposite*). This great hall of the Norman kings of
England mercifully survived the fire of 1834 and the
bombs of the 1939-45 war. It has been described as
'the finest timber-roofed building in Europe' and even
by modern standards the immense span of the timber
hammerbeam roof, which weighs over 600 tons, seems
to defy gravity. The hall was originally built by
William Rufus in 1097-99, but a simpler roof was then
supported on pillars. The remodelling, with the
hammerbeam roof, was carried out by Richard II from
1394 to 1401. His mason was Henry Yevele (see page
19, top) and the brilliant carpenter, who built the roof,
was Hugh Herland.

The Crypt, or lower chapel, of St Stephen's, Westminster (*right*). This is one of the few buildings of the Palace of Westminster that survived the fire of 1834, which destroyed the upper chapel over it. It was built in the late 13th and early 14th centuries, but would probably not be recognised by its builders because it was 'restored' by ruthless 19th-century busybodies. It is still used as a chapel by Members of Parliament.

Looking across the Thames to the Houses of Parliament (*above*). When the Palace of Westminster was destroyed by fire, in 1834, English architectural taste was divided between the merits of classical and Gothic design. (See page 15.) The work of reconstruction was finally entrusted to Charles Barry, who had won a competition calling for plans in the Gothic or Tudor style, though he had previously been successful with classical buildings, notably the Travellers Club. He employed the ardent Gothicist, Augustus Pugin, to design most of the decorative detail, and Pugin drew inspiration partly from Henry VII's chapel in Westminster Abbey. (See pages 20–21.)

The House of Lords: the Princes' Chamber. Pugin is
again the guiding genius of the decoration, but the
statue of Queen Victoria, which dominates the room,
is by John Gibson, 1854. The panel in bronze relief
over the fireplace is by Theed.

The House of Lords: the Royal Gallery. Pugin at his
most exuberant, with a lavish use of encaustic tiling in
red, blue and buff. The forty-five-foot long frescoes on
the side-walls are by Maclise, and show the death of
Nelson at Trafalgar and the meeting of Wellington
and Blücher on the field of Waterloo.

Tower of London: the White Tower (*right*). This Norman keep (see page 12 and page 14) was built inside London's Roman Walls, though part of the rest of the fortress extends outside them. That may account for the legend, current even in Shakespeare's day, that the Tower was built by Caesar. The only comparable Norman keep is at Colchester, also a Roman stronghold.

Foot Guards at the Tower (*opposite*). The presence of a detachment of Guards at the Tower of London is purely ceremonial, but is a reminder of the essentially military purpose which caused the fortress to be built, and kept it in good repair for nine centuries.

Tower of London: the Chapel of St John, in the White Tower (*right*). Pevsner describes it as 'one of the most impressive pieces of Early Norman architecture in England, very massive, and not relieved by ornamentation', by which he means architectural ornamentation; in its heyday it would have been filled with colour, and not nearly as austere and forbidding as it looks now.

The Crown Jewels (*opposite, top*). John Stow, writing in the reign of Elizabeth I, recorded that one of the functions of the Tower of London was to be a 'Treasurie of the ornaments and jewels of the Crowne', which it still is. Shown here are the Sovereign's Orb, and one of the Queen's sceptres – there are six sceptres in all. The English regalia are not old in historical terms, because Cromwell sold or melted down most of the older insignia of royalty. The oldest, St Edward's Crown, used in Coronations, was made for that of Charles II.

The Yeomen of the Guard (*above*): the oldest military unit in Britain, formed in 1485 by Henry VII immediately after his victory at Bosworth. It was recruited from those who were 'Yeomen and Gentlemen below the rank of Esquire'. Unlike some other old regiments the Yeomen did not break their continuity during the Civil War, because they served Charles II in exile and returned with him at the Restoration. Their last active service (discounting the air raids in the Second World War) was at the battle of Dettingen in 1743, in which George II took part. The special branch of the Yeomen of the Guard who do duty at the Tower of London, the Yeomen Warders, or 'Beefeaters', was formed by Henry VIII.

Military Ceremony at the Tower (*below*). Every evening in the Tower of London the Chief Warder of the Yeomen Warders, with his escort, takes part in the Ceremony of the Keys, which has been repeated daily without a break for at least seven centuries. In the pool of silence that the high walls of the Tower preserve within the hum of London, it is still probably the most impressive military ceremony in the world.

St Bartholomew the Great, Smithfield (*opposite*). The church and St Bartholomew's Hospital were founded in 1123 as an Augustinian priory by a courtier of Henry I, Rahere, as an act of piety. Only a small part of the original church remains; like other monastic churches in London it was 'quarried' after the Reformation, but is said to have London's earliest pointed arches on Norman pillars. 'Barts', the hospital, has of course survived.

Richard Coeur-de-Lion. The bronze statue of Richard I, by Marochetti, was put up in Old Palace Yard – that is to say, in the space between Parliament and the Abbey – in 1860. The sword was bent by a bomb splinter in the 1939-45 war but was subsequently straightened.

Charing Cross. Eleanor crosses, of which this is one, were erected to mark the places where the body of Eleanor of Castile (see page 19, bottom), Edward I's Queen, rested on its way to Westminster Abbey from Harby in Nottinghamshire. The original Charing cross, a few yards away, was taken down in 1647. This 19th-century one was designed by Barry.

Eltham Palace, as only the birds might have seen it in Plantagenet times. Eltham, in Kent, though it is now a suburb, was once far enough away from London for it to be a favourite country retreat for Plantagenet and later monarchs. Little has survived except the late-15th-century Great Hall, and that has had a chequered career: Turner painted it in use as a barn, and it was later a drill-hall. It was sympathetically restored, mainly in the 1930s, and is now open to the public.

Eltham Palace – the Bridge. Before Eltham became a Plantagenet palace it was a moated manor, the Bishop of Durham having bought it at the end of the 13th century from William de Vesci. The bridge across the moat, seen here, was shown still in use in an engraving of 1735 by Samuel and Nathaniel Buck, together with an elaborate gatehouse and the Great Hall.

The Lord Mayor's Coach at the Law Courts (*below*).
The new Lord Mayor drives here annually in
November, in the Lord Mayor's Show, to present
himself to the Lord Chief Justice, representing the
Monarch. He is attended by his guard of the Company
of Pikemen and Musketeers, provided by veterans of
the Honourable Artillery Company in 17th-century
uniform. The H.A.C. is still an active unit in the
Territorial Army, and the Queen is its
Captain-General.

Guildhall: the Great Hall (*opposite*). The centre of
municipal government of the City of London has
shown a capacity for survival typical of London itself.
The Hall was built in the first half of the 15th century,
but was badly damaged in the two Great Fires of 1666
and 1940. Inevitably it has been much rebuilt and
restored, but fortunately by sympathetic hands –
principally George Dance the Younger and
Giles Gilbert Scott.

The Baynard Castle (*below, left*). Baynard's Castle,
guarding the south-western corner of old London's river
frontage, where the River Fleet joined the Thames,
was to the Normans almost as important as the Tower.
Nothing has survived of the Norman fortification, but
in 1972 remains of the Baynard's Castle of Tudor times
(*below, right*) were uncovered during excavation for a
new building on Upper Thames Street. That was the
remains of Henry VII's version of Baynard's Castle,

which survived into the 17th century and is shown in river views of London of that time. Now only a pub preserves the name. A tablet on the wall of the pub explains that the Tudor castle was destroyed in the Great Fire of 1666, 'although remnants remained until the 19th century, when the present public house was constructed'. Charles II dined with the Earl of Shrewsbury in Baynard's Castle only a few days before the Great Fire. (See page 12.)

St James's Palace: Henry VIII's Gatehouse (*below*). Built about 1530, it has a noticeable kinship to the gatehouse on the West Front of Hampton Court Palace, and to Lupton's gatehouse at Eton, both of the same period. It guards the northern entrance to St James's Palace, looking up St James's Street, which is generally thought of as the acme of London urbanity; yet a commentator in Elizabeth I's reign wrote that the palace had 'a farme house opposite to its north gate', which was the gate seen here.

Bandsmen at St James's Palace (*bottom*). The five regiments of Foot Guards can be distinguished by the plumes on their bearskins, but for the layman more simply by the grouping of their tunic buttons: single buttons, Grenadiers; groups of two buttons, Coldstream; buttons in threes, Scots Guards; in fours, Irish Guards; in fives, Welsh Guards.

St James's Palace: the Tapestry Room (*below*). The room retains its original fireplace but was redecorated in 1866 by William Morris. Pevsner comments: 'It remains a most remarkable fact that such early recognition was given here to a new style which, in its day, was as revolutionary as the modern style was in England in 1935.'

St James's Palace: the Chapel Royal (*opposite*). The Chapel, like the Gatehouse, dates from the 1530s. Annually on January 6th (Epiphany) two Gentlemen Ushers offer gold, frankincense and myrrh here on behalf of the Sovereign. Charles I attended service here before he was executed; and among many royal weddings have been those of William and Mary, Queen Anne, George IV, and Queen Victoria and Prince Albert.

The Royal College of Surgeons, Lincoln's Inn Fields. The building, of 1835–36, is principally by Barry. Among its treasures, in the Hunterian Museum, is this recently restored cartoon (*above*) for Holbein's painting of Henry VIII with the Barber-Surgeons. There are also three paintings by Stubbs, of a rhinoceros, a baboon and a Macaque monkey, and portraits by Hogarth and Reynolds. The surgeons separated themselves from the barbers as recently as 1745.

Hampton Court from the air. Nearest the camera, and standing out plainly from the rest, is Wren's work, carried out for William and Mary. Beyond and left are the Tudor courts, and beyond the Great Gatehouse is Outer Green Court, and the Trophy Gates close to Hampton Court Bridge. The surviving Tudor building adjoining Wren's East Front is the Tennis Court. William III's formal gardens extend eastward towards Hampton Court Park and to the Thames, which swings round the palace in a wide arc.

Statue of Sir Thomas More (*below*), outside the More Chapel, Chelsea Old Church, where he used to worship. Nearby is Crosby Hall, on the garden of More's house in Chelsea. The Hall formerly stood in Bishopsgate, where it was built by a wool-merchant, Sir John Crosby, in the latter part of the 15th century, and was rented, briefly, by Richard III and by Sir Thomas More in the 1520s. It was taken down, moved to Chelsea in 1910 and incorporated in the 1927 Crosby Hall, a hostel of the British Federation of University Women.

Hampton Court Palace: the Great Gatehouse (*right*). Cardinal Wolsey bought the manor from the knights of St John of Jerusalem in 1514 and set about building the most splendid private house of his time. That incurred the jealousy of Henry VIII and, though Wolsey presented Hampton Court to the King in 1529, it probably contributed to Wolsey's downfall. The moat by the Great Gatehouse was filled up in 1690 and dug out again in 1910. The King's Beasts seen in the photograph are modern. Beyond the Gatehouse are the Tudor Clock Court, with the astronomical clock put in in 1540 and still going, and, further on, the Tennis Court built by Henry VIII.

Hampton Court Palace: the Great Hall. Here
Henry VIII and subsequent monarchs dined and
presided over state banquets, and it is still occasionally
so used. The hammerbeam roof is outstanding for its
rich ornamentation; the Brussels tapestries were made
in Henry VIII's time; the stone in the floor was once
the fireplace. George I used the Great Hall as a theatre.

Hampton Court Palace: the Pond Gardens. The gardens at Hampton Court, nearly all open to the public, cover an exceptionally wide range of tastes and periods, reflecting the pleasure that many kings and queens have taken in living there. Among the general public, perhaps the most popular is the Maze.

Hatfield Palace, Hertfordshire: the Great Hall. When the Cecils began to build Hatfield House in 1611, they 'quarried' stone from Hatfield Palace, built from 1496 onwards, and which in the next century was coveted and acquired as a royal palace by Henry VIII. Queen Elizabeth I spent much of her childhood at Hatfield, and it was here that she received the Earls of Pembroke and Arundel to tell her that she was Queen. All that now remains is the Great Hall, restored by the Marquess of Salisbury early in the present century.

Richmond Palace: the Gatehouse (*above*). This gateway, and Wardrobe Court in Old Palace Yard, are all that remain of Richmond Palace, and it is hard to realise that in Tudor England it was of great size and importance, though not as big as Hampton Court. There had been a royal residence at Richmond, then known as Shene, since Edward I's day, but it was burned down, and was rebuilt in 1498 by Henry VII, whose arms are over the Gatehouse. He called it Richmond because he had been Earl of Richmond in Yorkshire. Henry VII died at Richmond Palace, as did Elizabeth I.

Trumpeter's House, Richmond. It was built in 1714 by Richard Hill, brother of Abigail Hill, a friend of Queen Anne, on the site of the Middle Gate of Richmond Palace. Prince Metternich lived here for a time, when it was confusingly known as the Old Palace, and was visited by Disraeli, who described it in a letter to his sister as 'the most charming house in the world'.

Cricket on Richmond Green (*below*). The Gatehouse (page 52) faces Richmond Green where, according to local legend, Henry VIII jousted. I know of no evidence to confirm this, but it may well be true. At least we know that after Henry's death the Green was 'a piece of level turf of 20 acres, planted with 113 elms'. Forty-eight were on the west side, forming 'a hansome walk'.

Doorway in Maids of Honour Row, Richmond (*above*). Maids of Honour Row, or the Maids of Honour as it was formerly called, is described in Janet Dunbar's *A Prospect of Richmond* as 'an exceedingly elegant set of four houses built in 1723, by command of George I, for the accomodation of the ladies of the Court in attendance on the Princess of Wales, as there was no suitable accomodation for them elsewhere in the town'. The Prince and Princess of Wales (Caroline of Anspach) were then living at Richmond Lodge.

Deer in Richmond Park (*right*). Richmond Park, once known as the New Park, covers land that has been hunted by English kings for many centuries. In the reign of Henry VIII it was still known as Shene Chase, retaining the name of the precursor of Richmond Palace; but it was a later monarch, Charles I, who enclosed the Park with a wall, expressly for hunting deer in it.

Sixteenth-century London at Staple Inn (*opposite*).
These houses on the south side of Holborn are
generally regarded as the last remaining examples of
Elizabethan domestic architecture in London, but it is
fair to add that they have been much restored, first in
the late 19th century and then in 1937, when they
were reconstructed from behind in order to maintain
the Elizabethan fronts. However, Pevsner, not given to
lavishing praise on such restorations, bestows on them
the accolade of 'no doubt the most impressive
surviving example of timber building in London'.

Queen Elizabeth I in Fleet Street. This contemporary
statue of her stands on the outside wall of St Dunstan-
in-the-West, but it was originally over the old
Ludgate, the City's western gateway. The statue was
made about 1586 by William Kerwin.

Mary, Queen of Scots, in Fleet Street. She gives her
name to Queen of Scots House, No's 143-144, a
building not admired by Pevsner, who remarks:
'tastelessly and mercilessly Gothic.'

The Queen's House, Greenwich (*left*). In 1613 King James I gave the Tudor and pre-Tudor Palace of Placentia at Greenwich to Anne of Denmark, his Queen. She, wanting something more modern and easier to maintain, commissioned Inigo Jones to build her a house that is now admired as the earliest example of Palladian domestic architecture in England. It was on the site of this house that Raleigh spread his cloak to save Queen Elizabeth from stepping in the mud.

The Queen's House, Greenwich: the Tulip Staircase (*below*). The delicate Palladian staircase, with no inner supports, gets its name from the balustrade of wrought iron, with a top resembling a series of tulips, as can be seen in this photograph.

Somerset House: the Courtyard (*below*). Somerset House is now primarily the Inland Revenue and the Probate Registry, but many people feel that that is a waste of splendid building and site. It contains fine rooms designed for display and public use, which once housed the Royal Academy, the Royal Society and the Society of Antiquaries, whose names can still be found inscribed over the door inside the main entrance.

Somerset House at night, from the South Bank (*opposite*). The present Somerset House was built by William Chambers from 1776, expressly to house learned societies and public administrative offices. It stands on the site, however, of a palace built from 1547 by Edward Seymour, Duke of Somerset, Protector of the Realm during the reign of the boy King Edward VI. When Mary succeeded Edward she gave Somerset House to her half-sister Elizabeth, who used it for entertaining when she became Queen. James I gave the house to Anne of Denmark, who employed Inigo Jones to carry out major improvements. Anne of Denmark's son, Charles I, in turn gave the house to his Queen, the French Princess Henrietta Maria. She returned there as Queen Mother after the Restoration, and at her death Charles II gave it to his Queen, Catherine of Braganza. She was ultimately turned out by William and Mary – or more precisely by Mary – and the house gradually fell into disuse.

St James's Park in summer and winter. What had once been a marsh was drained by Henry VIII to provide a park for his palace, St James's, but it was Charles II who gave the park something of its present shape and opened it for public enjoyment. The winding banks of the lake were designed by Nash in 1828. The park is a great place to see water birds; including exotic ones, but perhaps, when the marsh was drained, conservationists complained that it would destroy the bird-life.

64

Prince Henry's Room, Fleet Street (*opposite*). Tradition links this room, over the entrance to Inner Temple Lane, with the eldest son of James I, who died in 1612. The building is old enough for that to be true, and there was on the original ceiling, now restored, the Prince of Wales's feathers and the monogram P.H. As Godfrey Thompson's revision of Kent's *London for Everyman* points out, however, that may refer only to the Prince's Arms tavern, which was on this site at about the date of Prince Henry's death.

Apothecaries' Hall, Blackfriars Lane (*left*). The Company of Apothecaries was incorporated by James I, and the members were originally tradesmen who sold remedies. Later they also prescribed, which involved them in a long legal struggle with the Royal College of Physicians, which they finally won by a judgement in the House of Lords in 1721.

Mulberries in Charterhouse Square (*below*). A Carthusian Priory was founded here in 1371. After the Dissolution it became a private house, and Elizabeth I and James I were among monarchs entertained in it. In 1611 Thomas Sutton founded Charterhouse School in the buildings, where the school remained until it moved to Godalming in 1872. The planting of mulberries for silkworm cultivation was keenly encouraged by James I.

Charles I in Trafalgar Square. This splendid bronze equestrian statue is by Le Sueur, 1633. It is Le Sueur's best-known work in London, though there are fine monuments by him in Westminster Abbey. Under Cromwell the statue was sold to a brazier, who was supposed to destroy it but fortunately buried it instead.

Speaker's Corner, Hyde Park. Hyde Park, extending to some 360 acres, was originally land belonging to the Abbey of Westminster, but at the Dissolution it was appropriated by Henry VIII as a royal deer-park. In 1635 Charles I opened the park to the public.

Band of the Scots Guards. Of the five regiments of
Foot Guards, the Scots Guards trace their origin to
1642, when Charles I issued letters patent to the
Marquess of Argyll to command a regiment of 1,500
men. They later took part in the battle of Dunbar
(1650) in Leslie's army, which was defeated by
Cromwell, and served under Prince Charles (later
Charles II) at the battle of Worcester, where they were
all but annihilated, Prince Charles escaping to France.
After the Restoration, in May, 1662, Charles II formed
a new regiment, the Third Foot Guards, of 600
soldiers, their Colours being 'red with a saltire of St
Andrew's Cross argent in a field azure'.

The Banqueting House, Whitehall (*below*). Inigo
Jones began work on this building in 1619, just after
the Queen's House at Greenwich (see pages 58-9) so it
ranks as the second example of Palladian architecture in
England and the first in London. The design is based
on Inigo Jones's study of Palladio's villas and palaces at
Vicenza, and it was part of what was then Whitehall
Palace. The building has been restored many times,
and in 1829 Soane refaced it in Portland stone in place
of Inigo Jones's Oxford and Northamptonshire stone.
It is still accepted as one of the most perfectly
proportioned buildings in Britain. Charles I was
executed in 1649 on a scaffold outside the first floor of
the Banqueting House.

The Banqueting House, Whitehall (*opposite*). This
magnificent hall is an exact double-cube, 55 ft. by
55 ft. by 110 ft. Charles I commissioned Rubens to paint
the ceiling, and it was completed in 1635. The ceiling
depicts the apotheosis of James I, together with
Religion, Zeal, Justice, Honour and Victory. One of
the panels shows Minerva driving out Rebellion, a sad
irony in view of King Charles's subsequent fate.

CHARLES II
By Caius Gabriel Cibber (1681)
Restored to the Square
by
LADY GILBERT IN 1938

Charles II in Soho Square (*opposite*). Soho Square was created in 1681 on the site of Monmouth House and was then called King Square. The statue of Charles II is by Cibber, 1681, and was, as the tablet tells us, restored to the square in 1938.

Oak-Apple Day at the Royal Hospital, Chelsea (*below*). In 1682 Charles II founded the Hospital, which Wren designed, as a home for former soldiers. Every year on May 29, Oak-Apple Day, the Pensioners wear oakleaves to celebrate Charles's escape in the Boscobel oak after the battle of Worcester.

St Paul's Cathedral (*opposite*). After Old St Paul's was destroyed in the Great Fire of 1666 there was prolonged debate about the nature of the cathedral that should replace it, and Wren's original design was criticised, on liturgical grounds, as unsuited to Church of England services. It was through the support of Charles II that Wren was able to proceed with the cathedral as it stands, the accepted masterpiece of English baroque.

St Paul's Cathedral: looking up to the Dome (*above*). Pevsner writes, of the Dome, 'the achievement of a final repose far more convincing than St Peter's'. What is seen, looking up, is the inner of three domes. Between it and the outer dome is a brick cone designed to carry the weight of the Lantern. Below the Dome can be seen the Whispering Gallery.

The Queen's Life Guard. The two regiments of the
Household Cavalry, the Life Guards and the Blues and
Royals, originate from the early years of the reign of
Charles II. The Life Guards wear scarlet tunics, the
Blues and Royals blue tunics. Both wear steel cuirasses,
and steel helmets with horse-hair plumes coloured
white for the Life Guards, crimson for the
Blues and Royals seen here.

James II in Trafalgar Square. He stands outside the
National Gallery looking, on a winter day, somewhat
underdressed for the occasion. The fine bronze statue is
by Grinling Gibbons, 1686, and was originally
intended to stand in Whitehall, though for a time it
was in St James's Park. The matching statue outside
the National Gallery is, incongruously, George
Washington, by Houdon.

William III in St James's Square (*left*). The Square is one of the oldest in London, but surprisingly the bronze statue is not of William's era; it was made in 1807 and is by Bacon. There is a touch of irony, bearing in mind that William III died after a fall from a horse, that he should be depicted mounted, whereas Charles II and James II (pages 70 and 75) are both seen by Londoners standing firmly on their feet.

The Chapel of the Royal Naval College, Greenwich (*below, left*). When William and Mary decided to live at Hampton Court rather than at Greenwich, Wren was invited to design a Naval Hospital on the site of the old Greenwich Palace of Placentia, to correspond with the Royal Hospital for retired soldiers in Chelsea. The chapel was partly destroyed by fire in 1779 and restored under the supervision of 'Athenian' Stuart. The massive painting behind the altar is by Benjamin West.

Ceiling of the Painted Hall at Greenwich (*below*). Thornhill's allegorical painting shows King William receiving an olive branch from Peace, while Concord attends Queen Mary. Tyranny, appropriately, lies under the King's feet. The charioteer driving about above them is Apollo. Those at the Royal Naval College who dine in these splendid surroundings, however, find it difficult to take it all in and eat dinner at the same time.

Queen Anne's Gate. The houses in the Queen Square end of what is now Queen Anne's Gate date from her reign. Pevsner writes of them: 'the ensemble of houses of uniform design surviving from that time is better than anything else of the same kind and date in London.' Queen Anne herself surveys the scene from outside No 15.

St Mary-le-Strand. There has been a church on this site since the 12th century, though Protector Somerset pulled one of them down in 1549 to provide stone for his Somerset House. This familiar London landmark, on an island in the traffic of the Strand, is by James Gibbs and dates from the last year of the reign of Queen Anne, the first of the fifty churches that she ordered to be built.

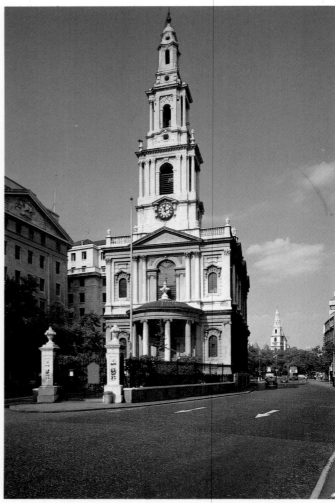

Fortnum and Mason (*opposite*). The building, of 1926-27, is described, slightly acidly, by Pevsner as 'in the style that has earned American approval in Grosvenor Square'. Fortnums was going strongly in the reign of George III and supplied groceries to Queen Caroline. The firm was founded in 1707 by Hugh Mason and William Fortnum, who began by selling candles; Mr Fortnum had previously been a footman at the Court of Queen Anne. The clock, a Piccadilly landmark, is as recent as 1964. The two figures, Mr F. and Mr M., appear on each hour carrying respectively a candelabra and a tray of tea. Meanwhile the clock plays the Eton Boating Song – though I am not sure why.

St Martin-in-the-Fields (*opposite*). Although it lies well outside the old Walls of London, there has been a church here since the early 13th century, which was replaced by one built by Henry VIII, and that in its turn was replaced in 1721 by the present fine building, by James Gibbs. George I's arms are over the portico, to indicate that the king contributed to the cost. Visitors who are told that Winston Churchill is buried here look surprised, but the statement is correct. It refers however to the first Winston, father of the great Duke of Marlborough. The equestrian statue in Trafalgar Square shows George IV riding, somewhat improbably, bareback.

The Royal Mews, Buckingham Palace (*above*). The Mews and the Queen's Gallery are the only parts of the Palace that are open to the public. Times of admission to the Mews are usually to be found posted near the gates. Among the coaches and carriages to be seen are the Great State Coach, shown here, built in 1761 for George III and used since to carry the monarch to his or her coronation. It was designed by Sir William Chambers and is decorated with paintings by the Florentine, Giambattista Cipriani. Other notable coaches are the Irish State Coach and the Glass Coach, used at royal weddings.

Hyde Park. The Serpentine, which runs
through Hyde Park from Kensington Gardens, where
it is called the Long Water, was made by damming the
Westbourne; the suggestion that the lake should be
made came from George III's Queen, Caroline. When
the Westbourne leaves the Park it disappears
underground on its way to the Thames, though it
makes a final brief public appearance in a large pipe
over the platforms of Sloane Square station. There is a
fine bridge over the Serpentine, where it joins the
Long Water, by George Rennie, 1826.

Feeding the Birds: the Serpentine. Feeding the birds is
a daily ritual here and in St James's Park. Near
Rennie's bridge is a bird sanctuary, with Epstein's
statue of Rima, a character out of the novel, *Green
Mansions*, by the naturalist, W. H. Hudson, to whom
the statue is a memorial. Among Hudson's other books
is *Birds in London* (1898). Epstein's statue caused fierce
controversy when it was put up and still divides
opinion sharply.

The British Museum.
When the great physician
and scientist Sir Hans
Sloane died in 1753 he
left his collection of
books, manuscripts and
antiquities to the nation,
and they were displayed
in what was then
Montague House in
Bloomsbury. Later the
Elgin Marbles, the
Townley Marbles and
other antiquities were
added, and it was decided
in 1821 that Robert
Smirke should be
commissioned to build a
museum to house the
growing collection, to
which in 1823 was added
George III's library.

The British Museum
The British Library
Reference Division

The Life Guards at Hyde Park Corner (*below*). In the early 19th century the road junction that we now call Hyde Park Corner was thought of as the western entrance to the capital, which explains why the Duke of Wellington called Apsley House 'No 1, London'. In 1825 Decimus Burton was commissioned to build a Constitution Arch at the top of Constitution Hill. At one time the arch was surmounted by an equestrian statue of the Iron Duke, but it was replaced in 1912 by Victory driving a quadriga, by Adrian Jones.

The Royal Society of Arts (*opposite*). In 1753, when the Society was founded, William Shipley, one of the founders, wrote that 'encouragement is much the same to Arts and Sciences as culture to vegetables; they always advance and flourish in proportion to the rewards they acquire and the honours they obtain.' The Society has a long list of royal Presidents, including Prince Albert in 1843 and the Duke of Edinburgh since 1952. Its splendid building in John Adam Street is the largest of the remaining blocks of the original Adelphi, and among the most important examples of the Adam Brothers' work in London. Part of the building has been occupied by the Society since its completion in 1774, and is the first building erected in England as the headquarters of a learned society.

Kew Palace. This, the oldest of the royal buildings in Kew Gardens, was previously known first as the Prince's House and then as Kew Palace. It is exceptional not only among English palaces but among buildings of its period in that it has hardly been altered since its construction in 1631. In the 18th century it was a favourite royal residence, particularly as a summer home for George III. It was from this house that the Prince of Wales, later the Prince Regent, enjoyed secret meetings at night in the garden with 'Perdita', the actress Mary Robinson. She is said to have been smuggled in through a hole in the garden wall.

Kew Palace: the Queen's Drawing Room (*below*, *right*). This, the most important room in the Palace, is on the first floor, over the King's Dining Room. Kew Palace has a long association with Royal Family music-making; Mercer's celebrated *Music Party* of 1733 shows Frederick, Prince of Wales, playing the cello there in a family trio with his sisters.

Kew Palace: the Garden (*bottom*). What are now generally known as Kew Gardens are in fact two separate gardens joined together: the garden of Kew House, where Chambers designed the Orangery; and that of Richmond Lodge, with its Long Lake by Capability Brown. They were made into the Royal Botanic Gardens in 1840.

Kew Gardens: the Thatched Lodge. A lively account
of the homely routine at Kew Palace in the time of
George III has been left by Mrs Papendiek, wife of a
court official. She records that Queen Charlotte had a
cottage, roofed with thatch, built for her personal use
in the Gardens, and that she liked to take tea there.

Kew Gardens: the Chinese Pagoda. Kew offers the visitor exotica in buildings as well as plants. The Chinese Pagoda, 165-foot and ten-storeys high, was designed by William Chambers, the architect of Somerset House (pages 60-61), and is the most celebrated local landmark. It commands a magnificent view from the top. There is also a Japanese gateway, a replica from the Buddhist temple of Nishi Hongwanji, and a tall flagstaff of Douglas fir from British Columbia.

Lancaster House: the South Front. Now used for
Government hospitality, Lancaster House, which has
also been called York House and Stafford House, was
built by Wyatt from 1825 for the then Duke of York
– the grand old duke who 'had ten thousand men; He
marched them up to the top of the hill, And marched
them down again.' When Queen Victoria visited the
Duchess of Sutherland here, she is quoted as saying: 'I
come from my house to your palace' – which perhaps
reminded the Duchess of Henry VIII at Wolsey's
Hampton Court.

Lancaster House: the Staircase. Basically it follows
Wyatt's plans but was modified by Barry when he
took over from Wyatt as architect. Pevsner admires
the 'sumptuous design and colouring' and remarks on
the 'equally sumptuous and very heavy cast-iron
balustrade'. Lancaster House, in Stable Yard, is part of
the St James's Palace complex of royal buildings. At
one time it housed the London Museum.

The Royal Opera Arcade (*above*). Confusingly, it is nowhere near the present Royal Opera House but runs from Charles II Street to Pall Mall. It was built by Nash in 1816 and is the oldest of the capital's arcades; it is odd that shopping arcades were not developed earlier and that there are not more of them in London, bearing in mind the wet climate. This one has shops on the west side only, unlike the Burlington Arcade, built a year or two later.

Carlton House Terrace. Though George IV is criticised for his architectural extravagance, often on buildings of such doubtful taste as the Royal Pavilion at Brighton, we also owe to his extravagance many architectural splendours, among them Carlton House Terrace. Designed by Nash, it provides the northern flank, for much of its distance, of London's ceremonial way, the Mall. (See page 15.)

The King's Troop, R.H.A., driving through the
Marble Arch. The Arch was designed by Nash as a
ceremonial entrance to Buckingham Palace, but has
stood in the north-east corner of Hyde Park since 1851.
The King's Troop was raised in 1946, at the express
wish of King George VI, as the Mounted Saluting
Battery, R.H.A., the Riding Troop; the rest of the
Royal Horse Artillery having been mechanised by
1939. It has retained the name, the King's Troop, in
George VI's memory.

Kensington Palace: Statue of Queen Victoria by her
daughter, Princess Louise, to commemorate fifty years
of her reign. Humbert Wolfe summed it up:
The shape's all wrong,
And the crown don't fit;
But – bless her old heart!
She was proud of it.

Kensington Palace: the South Front. In 1689 William
of Orange bought Nottingham House in Kensington
and commissioned Wren to adapt it as a palace. As
Pevsner remarks, never did a powerful monarch of the
age of Louis XIV build a less ostentatious palace. The
equestrian statue is of King William. Queen Victoria
was the last British sovereign to live here, though it
has remained a favourite London home for other
members of the Royal Family.

Kensington Palace. In this bedroom on the north-east side of the Palace was born on May 24, 1819, Princess Victoria, daughter to the Duke of Kent and his German wife, Victoria of Saxe-Coburg. They were delayed in Germany during the Duchess's pregnancy and only just got back to London in time for the princess to be born in England. Eight months later the Duke died, but Victoria remained at Kensington Palace with her mother.

Victoria and Albert Museum: the Courtyard. The
V. & A. is largely the brainchild of Prince Albert, but
the foundation stone of the present building was laid in
1899 by Queen Victoria. Foreign visitors to London,
accustomed to logic in the organisation of museums,
find it hard to distinguish between the functions of the
British Museum, the Tate and the V. & A. That is
because the three have grown up casually, and it takes
a lifetime in London to know what to find in which.
David Piper, a distinguished museum director, lists, for
the V. & A.: architectural detail; arms and armour; the
art of the book; bronzes; carpets; clocks; costume;
embroidery; enamels; engravings; fabric; furniture;
glass; gold; silver and ironwork; ivories; jewellery;
musical instruments; pottery and porcelain; tapestry;
theatre art; and woodwork. Not a bad list.

The Royal Opera House, Covent Garden: a production of *Aida*. The present building is the third. John Rich's theatre was destroyed by fire in 1808, but not before it had presented many of Handel's later works; the next opera house, by Smirke, suffered the fate of its predecessor in 1856. The present one, by Edward Barry (not Charles), dates from 1858. On this site have appeared great actors from Garrick to Macready; and great singers from Jenny Lind onwards.

Temple Bar and the Royal Courts of Justice (*opposite*). The memorial on the right marks the site of Wren's Temple Bar, which stood here until 1878, marking the western boundary of the City of London. Behind are the Royal Courts of Justice, by G. E. Street, 1882; earnest and complicated Victorian Gothic, but not related to any recognisable English tradition. As architecture the building has always been criticised; Galsworthy allowed one of his characters in the *Forsyte Saga* to remark that the Great Hall would make excellent rackets courts.

Lincoln's Inn. Looking from the early-15th-century Old Buildings through an archway to the fountain in New Square – one of the more agreeable survivals of the word 'new', since the very beautiful square is almost pure late-17th-century domestic architecture. A Queen's Counsel, or Q.C., can be distinguished from a barrister because he is entitled to wear a silk gown; being appointed a Q.C. is known as 'taking silk'.

Rendering of the Quit Rents by the Corporation of London. Every year in October, at the Royal Courts of Justice, the Comptroller and Solicitor of the City of London presents to the Queen's Remembrancer, on behalf of the Crown, a blunt knife and a sharp knife, and then six horseshoes and 61 nails, to represent the rendering of rents and services in respect of two parcels of land called the Moors, in Shropshire, and the Forge, in the parish of St Clement Danes. The ceremony dates from the 13th century; until recently, a billhook and a hatchet were present in place of the two knives.

The Victoria Memorial (*below*). At the Buckingham
Palace end of the Mall, it is part of the National
Memorial to Queen Victoria, together with the
Admiralty Arch which closes the Mall vista at the
Trafalgar Square end. It was designed by Thomas
Brock in 1911, though the surround in which it stands
is by Aston Webb, architect of the East Front of
Buckingham Palace. The white marble plinth supports
a gilt figure of Victory. On great occasions the
Memorial provides an unofficial grandstand outside the
Palace for those members of the public nimble enough
to climb it.

The Albert Memorial and the Albert Hall (*opposite*).
The Memorial was built between 1863 and 1872 by
George Gilbert Scott in a strange medley of styles and
materials at the then immense cost of £120,000.
Beneath the canopy Prince Albert sits holding the
catalogue of the Great Exhibition of 1851. The Albert
Hall, of the same dates, is by a succession of architects;
it seats 8,000 within its 735-foot girth. The glass and
iron dome carries on something of the spirit of
Paxton's lost Crystal Palace.

The Admiralty Arch. Like the East Front of
Buckingham Palace, and of almost the same date, it is
by Aston Webb, who was thus given an opportunity
to adorn London offered to few architects since the
rebuilding after the Great Fire; yet surprisingly few
Londoners or visitors to London even know his name.
At one time Winston Churchill, as First Lord of the
Admiralty, had a flat over the Arch.

Marlborough House: the South Front. It was designed
around 1710 by Wren as the London home of the first
Duke of Marlborough and Sarah, his Duchess, and the
Duke's body lay in state here. In 1817 the Prince
Regent bought the house, and it has since been, among
other uses, a royal dower house. Queen Mary lived
here after the death of George V and filled it with the
treasures of her collection. It is now the
Commonwealth Centre.

Marlborough House: the Blenheim Room. The present air of peace and elegance belies a stormy past; Sarah, Duchess of Marlborough, had her famous and final row with Queen Anne at Marlborough House, and Edward VII, when Prince of Wales, held some of his more flamboyant parties here. Among the paintings are Laguerre's scenes of the battle of Blenheim.

The Queen's Chapel, Marlborough Road (*opposite*).
Pevsner lists it as 'one of the few certain works of
Inigo Jones'. It must also be one of the most beautiful
chapels in England; it is open to the public for divine
service from Easter Day to the last Sunday in July.
Divine service is held in the Chapel Royal, St James's
Palace, from the first Sunday in October to Good
Friday. Charles I commissioned the Chapel for Queen
Henrietta Maria in 1623.

Memorial to Queen Alexandra, Marlborough Road
(*above*). This remarkable but little noticed *art nouveau*
bronze, on the garden wall of Marlborough House, is
by Alfred Gilbert, best known to Londoners, and all
over the world, for his Eros in Piccadilly Circus. It
deserves more attention than it gets.

Buckingham Palace from the air (*opposite*). Normally the gardens at the Palace, which cover some forty acres with a five-acre lake, are seen only by those members of the public lucky enough to be invited to a Garden Party. But a fleeting glimpse can be obtained from the top deck of a bus travelling south down Grosvenor Place.

Buckingham Palace from St James's Park (*left*). Aston Webb's East Front looking its most elegant and serene on a sunny spring morning. The serenity is usually disturbed by traffic gyrating round the Victoria Memorial. Pevsner terms that roundabout a *rond-point*, because of its 'Parisian, Beaux-Arts character'.

Changing Guard at Buckingham Palace (*left*). Not only Christopher Robin and Alice, but every tourist in London, pays a ritual visit that is as formalised, in its way, as the drill of the Guards themselves.

Regent's Park: Queen Mary's Gardens. Within the Inner Circle Road in Regent's Park lie Queen Mary's Gardens, at one time the property of the Royal Botanical Society but now open to the public; they are celebrated for their roses. Also within the Inner Circle is the Open Air Theatre – a delightful place to see a Shakespeare comedy on a fine summer evening.

White Lodge, Richmond Park. The house was built by
George II; George III had additions made by Wyatt,
and later the grounds were redesigned by Humphry
Repton. Edward VII lived here in his teens (and found
it dreadfully boring); Princess Mary of Teck lived here
as a girl; and when she married the Prince of Wales,
later George V, came back to her parents' home here
for the birth of her first son, later Edward VIII.

White Lodge: the Royal Ballet School. In 1955, White Lodge became the home of the Lower School of the Royal Ballet School. Pupils, mainly boarders, range from eleven to sixteen years of age and are drawn from all over Britain, with a few from abroad. The Upper School is at Baron's Court, and takes day-students from sixteen to nineteen years. The future home of the Upper School is part of the development scheme for the Royal Opera House in Covent Garden.

The King's Troop R.H.A. firing a salute in Hyde Park. A salute of forty-one guns is fired on the Queen's birthday and other state occasions. Corresponding salutes are fired by the Honourable Artillery Company from the Tower of London. The Royal Horse Artillery was formed in 1793 to provide artillery that was capable of keeping up with the cavalry.

Clarence House, St James's (*below*). Nash was commissioned to build Clarence House in 1825 for the Duke of Clarence, who was later to become William IV. Since then, however, it has been much changed, inside and out, and by the addition of a wing in 1873 linking it directly to St James's Palace. The present Queen, then Princess Elizabeth, lived here after her marriage, and here Princess Anne was born. Clarence House is now the London home of Queen Elizabeth the Queen Mother.

Wimbledon (*left*): the All-England Lawn Tennis and Croquet Club, to give it its full title. Tennis – the original game – has been a royal game since the Middle Ages, but lawn tennis can also claim royal favour: George VI was particularly fond of it and, as Duke of York, played in the Men's Doubles at Wimbledon in 1926. Oddly enough, Thomas Cromwell, minister to Henry VIII who was a renowned tennis player, lived near the present All-England Club, and Henry VIII created him Baron Wimbledon.

C. F. Trumper, of 9 Curzon Street, Court Hairdresser and Perfumer. A Royal Warrant of Appointment is a mark of recognition to an individual supplier of goods or services to the Queen, the Duke of Edinburgh, Queen Elizabeth the Queen Mother or the Prince of Wales. That warrant gives the firm the right to display the Royal Arms. Trumper's warrant to King George VI was replaced in 1977, and they now hold a warrant to Queen Elizabeth II. Royal Warrants have been granted since Hanoverian days, though not during the short reign of Edward VIII.

Bargemaster of the Fishmongers' Company. Many of the powers and privileges of the Livery Companies of the City of London (see also pages 43 and 65) date from the reign of Edward III, who himself was a member of the Merchant Taylors' Company. The senior companies, the 'Great Twelve', are: Mercers, Grocers, Drapers, Fishmongers, Goldsmiths, Skinners, Merchant Taylors, Haberdashers, Salters, Ironmongers, Vintners and Clothworkers. One of the roles still played by the ancient Livery Companies is to provide financial backing for schools, such as the Mercers to St Paul's School, the Merchant Taylors to Merchant Taylors' School and the Skinners to Tonbridge School.

The State Opening of Parliament. Annually Her Majesty the Queen drives from Buckingham Palace to the Palace of Westminster in the Irish State Coach. She is dressed in white, with a diamond tiara on her head and the blue riband of the Order of the Garter worn diagonally from her left shoulder. A Sovereign's Escort of the Household Cavalry rides with the coach. At one end of the Chamber of the House of Lords is the Throne. As the Queen leaves her carriage she is met by the Lord Great Chamberlain and the Earl Marshal, who conduct her to the Robing Room, where she puts

on the Parliament Robe and the Imperial State Crown, that Crown having already been brought from Buckingham Palace under cavalry escort together with the Sword of State (*above*). The Queen, having walked in procession to the Throne, sends Black Rod to bid the Speaker and Members of the Commons to attend her in the Upper Chamber. The Commons take their places at the Bar of the House. The Lord Chancellor kneels and hands the Queen a paper, from which she reads the Gracious Speech, opening that session of Parliament (*right*). The speech is, of course, not written by Her Majesty, but is an outline of what the Government intends to do in the session ahead.

Spencer House, St James's Place (*above*). A Palladian
town house built by John Vardy in the middle of the
18th century as the London home of the Earls Spencer,
the family of the Princess of Wales. The house, at the
time of writing, is occupied by the Economist
Intelligence Unit.

The Royal Festival Hall. London's first major post-1945 public building, on a site on the South Bank that was cleared for the 1951 Festival of Britain, it has become a much admired focus of the capital's musical life. Pevsner, writing in 1952 when the Hall was new, said, of the interior: 'Here . . . are a freedom and intricacy of flow, in their own way as thrilling as what we see in the Baroque churches of Germany and Austria.'

Acknowledgements

Author's Acknowledgements

In compiling this book I have drawn information from the
following, many of which are also acknowledged in the text:

A Prospect of Richmond, Janet Dunbar (White Lion)
Historic London, G. E. Eades (Queen Anne Press)
The Work of the Queen, Dermot Morrah (William Kimber)
Londinium, John Morris; revised by Sarah Macready (Weidenfeld
and Nicolson)
Royal Palaces, Castles & Homes, Patrick Montague-Smith and Hugh
Montgomery-Massingberd (Country Life Books)
The Buildings of England: London Vol I and II, Nikolaus Pevsner
(Penguin)
London: an Illustrated Companion Guide, David Piper (Collins)
Hanoverian London, George Rudé (Secker and Warburg)
London for Everyman, William Kent, revised by Godfrey Thompson
(Dent)

I am also grateful to Sarah Macready, Kenneth Whitehorne and
Mrs Elizabeth Eames for kindly reading and revising sections of the
text, and to J. N. P. Watson for checking my references to the
Household Cavalry. I am also particularly grateful to Patricia Pierce
and Margaret Saunders for their endless patience and hard work in
helping with the book. And I am indebted to Ernest Benn for
permission to quote Humbert Wolfe's verses from *Kensington
Gardens*.

Photographic Acknowledgements

The photographs on the following pages are reproduced by
Gracious Permission of Her Majesty The Queen: 11, 41, 42, 110.
The photograph on page 31 top is Crown copyright and is
reproduced with the permission of the Controller of Her Majesty's
Stationery Office.
Aerofilms, Boreham Wood 112; John Bethell, St Albans 17, 34–35,
38, 38–39, 46, 50–51, 52, 57, 61, 66 left, 68, 70, 75, 78 left, 78 right,
79, 86, 89 bottom, 90–91, 91, 94, 94–95, 100, 103, 104, 105, 107,
114–115, 116–117; British Tourist Authority, London 29, 40
bottom, 66 right, 67, 74–75, 81, 96, 101, 102 left, 113 bottom,
126–127; Camera Press, London – Peter Abbey 125; Colour Library
International, London 8, 18, 23, 24–25, 26, 27, 36, 37, 60, 62,
62–63, 76–77, 82–83, 84–85, 111, 113 top, 118–119, 120–121, 124;
Department of the Environment, London 13, 14, 22, 28 top, 31
bottom, 34, 44–45, 46–47, 48, 88–89, 89 top, 92, 97, 98, 98–99,
108–109; Tim Graham, London 2; Hamlyn Group Picture Library
19 bottom, 93, 117; Hamlyn Group – Catherine Blackie 16, 24, 33
right, 55 top, 65 top, 65 bottom, 80, 106, 121; Brian Hawkes,
Sittingbourne 49, 59, 77; Angelo Hornak, London 19 top, 20–21,
32, 40 top, 58–59, 64, 72, 73; Jarrold and Sons, Norwich 69; A. F.
Kersting, London 28 bottom, 126; Andrew Lawson, Charlbury 30,
56 left, 56 right, 70–71, 87, 102 right, 122–123, 123; Medical
Illustration Support Service, London 43; Mike Peters, Twickenham
54–55, 76 top, 83; Patricia Pierce, Sunbury-on-Thames 33 left,
52–53, 54.